INSIDER
TIPS & TRICKS

By Michael Ricks

TABLE OF CONTENTS

QUICK START
GETTING AROUND UNREAL ENGINE

Open up the Alien Spaceship Unreal Engine Project

Let's open up the project and start getting familiar with some of the basics. I'm going to be covering material as if you are brand new to Unreal Engine, so if you know all this already feel free to skip ahead.

The project should open up to the level with all the aliens on a concrete platform called:

Exile_Alien_Anims_MAP

You can download the scene here: https://michael-ricks.com/resources

Your screen should look something like this:

Navigate to the Animation Folder

Go to CONTENT > AlienSpaceship_Scene > Exile_Alien > Animation

Click on the animation folder and you will see the 28 motion capture alien animations:

Drag-And-Drop

Select one of the animations by left clicking on it, and while holding down the left mouse button, drag your character into the scene to the desired location and release the mouse button. Congratulations! You have just added your first character to the scene! Did you notice how Unreal Engine already has your character's feet level with the floor? Pretty cool!

Before we get the animation started, let's cover some basics on how to move around the interface.

How to get around the interface

Select your character by clicking on him. There will be a yellow outline around him to indicate he is selected. To deselect, press your escape key or click on another object such as the floor or sky. I prefer to use the escape key so nothing else is selected.

The "F" key is your best friend

It took me weeks before I finally figured this one out! To smoothly rotate around your character:

1. Select the character
2. Press the "F" key on your keyboard (this centers the focus on your character)
3. Press the "ALT" key on your keyboard while pressing the LEFT mouse button and moving your mouse. This will let you smoothly rotate around your object.
4. Remember, the "F", "ALT", and Left mouse button combo are your best friends!

Other important keyboard controls

- Middle mouse button - move left to right, up or down
- Scroll wheel - zoom in or out
- ALT + Left mouse button - zoom in out also
- Left mouse button + move mouse forward and back - zoom in and out also

Moving, rotating and scaling your character

- Select your character
- The indicator gizmo will show on your character
- Press the spacebar to toggle thru the move, rotate and scale controls
- You can also do this with the icons on the top of the screen

Let's get ready to animate

Go to the PLAY icon at the top of the screen and click on the small arrow pointing downward. Select SIMULATE from the drop down choices and exit the menu:

Press PLAY

Your character will start moving along with all of the other aliens in the scene. Congratulate yourself - you just set up your first successful animation! Be sure to press the STOP button before continuing to make editing changes. Spend some time playing around with the scene, moving characters around and getting familiar with how things work. Above all...have fun!

How to delete your character

Select your character and press the delete button on your keyboard. Your character will be deleted from the scene. He will still be there in the folder, so you can just drag-and-drop him back in the scene if you wish.

MAKE A PARAMETER FOR TEXTURE RESIZING
IN UNREAL ENGINE

Introduction

You know the situation - You have your cool model or object all set up and ready to go. You apply your material and the bricks or stones, or what-have-you is either too big or too small! So you search and search and try to find a way to **adjust the size of the texture** with no luck. *Believe me, I've been there.*

In this tutorial we're going to learn **EXACTLY** how to set this up to give us this power and flexibility. The cool thing is, that once we have it set up once, we can save it as a **MASTER**

MATERIAL and use it as a Template for all our future materials, creating as many different Material Instances as we want! Let's get started!

Import Starter Content Pack

From the Content Browser click the green **ADD NEW** button and go up to the very top where it says **ADD FEATURE OR CONTENT PACK**. Select that.

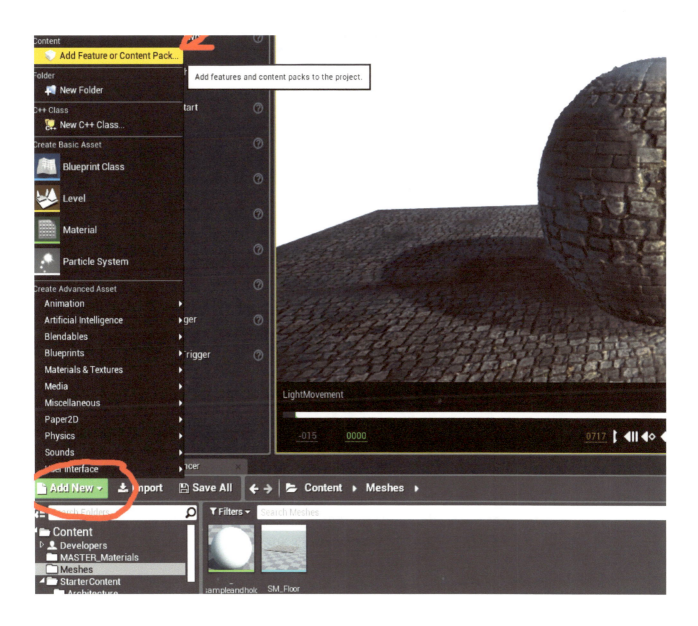

Add the Starter Content Pack to your scene:

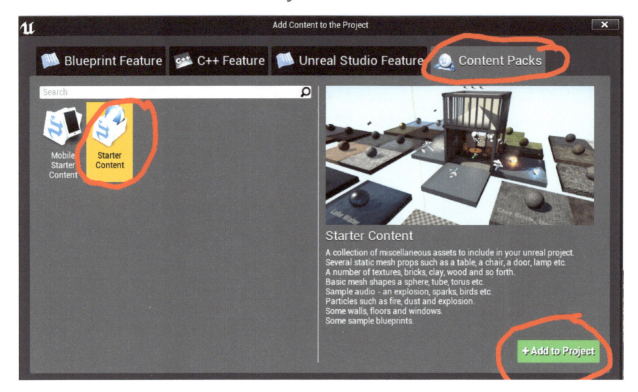

Click on the **Content Packs tab**, and select Starter Content. Then click **ADD TO PROJECT** and it will show up in your Content Browser.

Create a new Master Material

Right click in an empty area of the content browser and in the pop up menu select **MATERIAL**. This will create a new material that we will rename **MASTER_Brick_Clay_Old.**

Double click on your material to open up the Material Editor.

Next we need to drag in the following textures found in the **Starter Content > Textures** Folder into the Material Editor of the material you created:

- **T_Brick_Clay_Old_D** (Diffuse/Color Map)
- **T_Brick_Clay_Old_N** (Normal Map)

After you have our color and normal texture in your editor, hook them up to the **BASE COLOR** and **NORMAL** channels by **clicking and dragging from one to the other.** It will look like this:

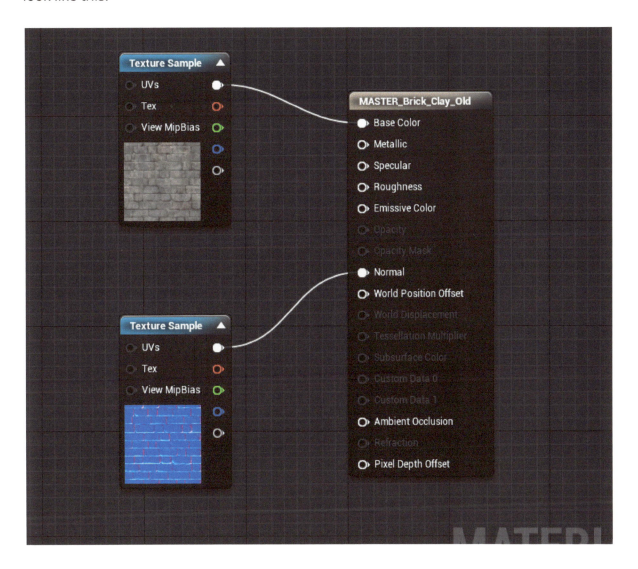

Let's add some Roughness and Metallic to the Material

Hold down the **"S" key on your keyboard while clicking with your left mouse button** and you will add a **Scalar Parameter.** You will do this **twice.** Name the first one **'roughness,'** and the second one **'metallic.'**

When you click on the node, look in the left hand panel and that's where you will find the Parameter Name and Default Value. For roughness let's put **0.6 for the value**. A value of 0 would be totally shiny and a value of 1 would be flat with no shine. You can adjust this to your liking. In the 'metallic' node let's **leave it at 0**.   Your node setup should now look like this:

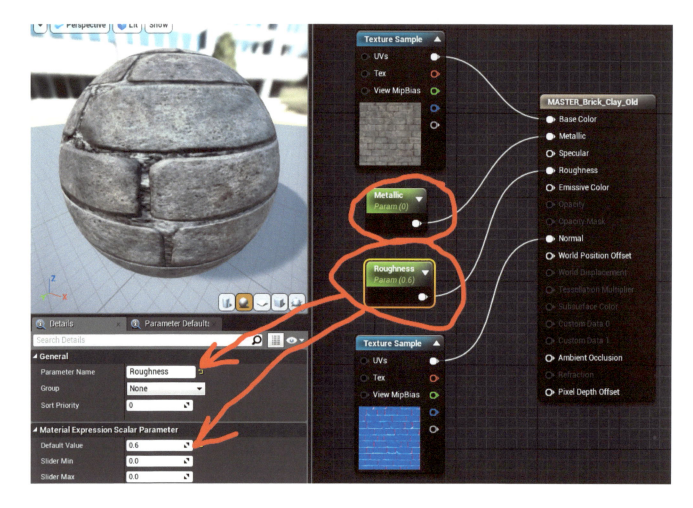

Let's convert the textures to parameters

You'll see soon why this is so important and handy to do. When we create Instances of our material, creating texture parameters will allow us to swap out the textures for other ones so we don't have to build all of this from scratch every time.

- First, click on the brick color texture so it is **highlighted**
- Then, **right click** on the node and a menu will pop up
- Select **CONVERT TO PARAMETER**
- Name the parameter **BRICK DIFFUSE**
- Do the same steps for the **normal map**

Select Texture Node, Right click and select 'Convert to Parameter'

When you've done these steps your node setup should look like this:

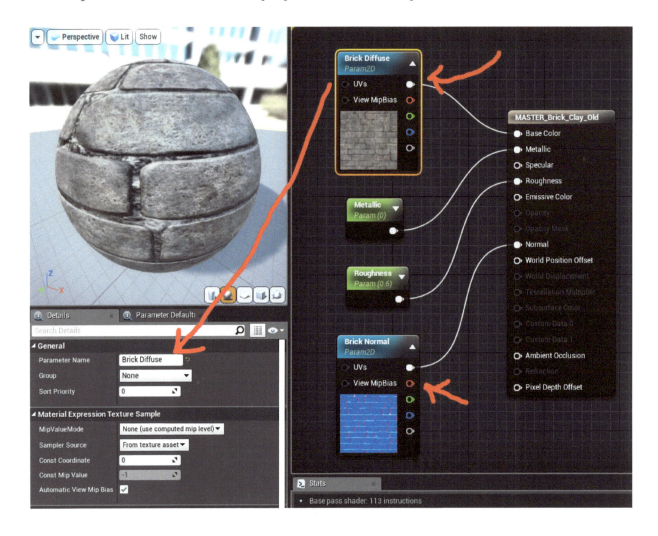

Creating our Texture Size Adjustment Parameter

This image shows how our completed node setup looks after we are finished setting up our texture coordinate nodes and hooking them up to our textures:

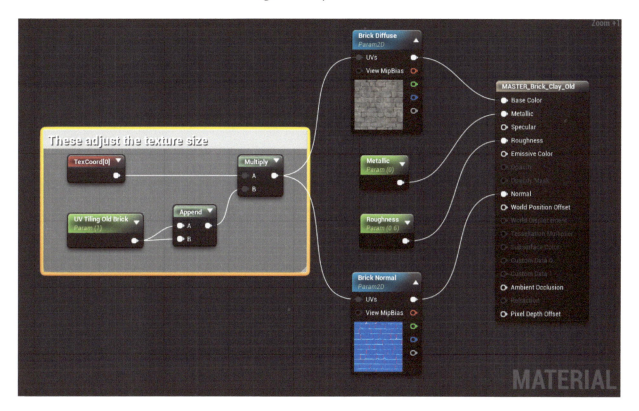

From the Material Editor Palette Section on the right side

This is where you will search for the needed nodes shown above in the yellow square. They are the following:

- TextureCoordinate
- ScalarParameter
- AppendVector
- Multiply

You will find them in the palette, using the search bar:

Now let's make an 'Instance' of our new Material!

First, let's be sure to **save our Material** so we don't lose all our hard work.

Go to your Content Browser where your Master Material is and click on:

MASTER_Brick_Clay_Old

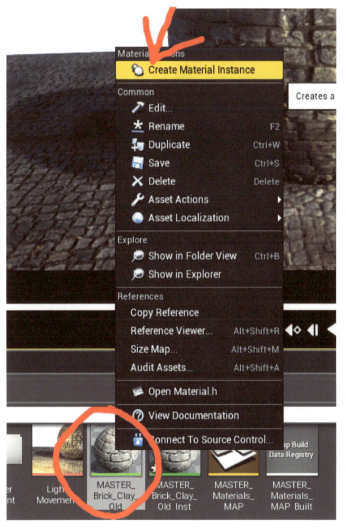

It should be ***highlighted in yellow***. Now **RIGHT CLICK** on the Material and a menu will pop-up. Select the very top option that says **CREATE MATERIAL INSTANCE.**

It will automatically add '_Inst' to the end of the Material name, which is fine for now. Your new Material Instance name is:

MASTER_Brick_Clay_Old_Inst

Double click on your Material Instance and let's take a look. You should see several Parameters that are grayed out that have check boxes in front of them.

Go ahead and click the check boxes so they become active.

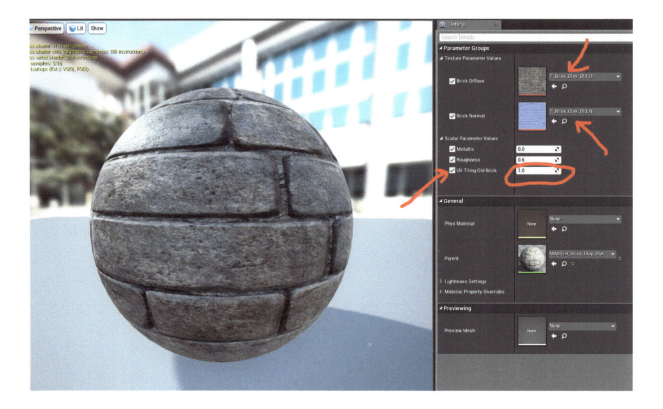

Study the above image and notice the following:

- The **Diffuse** & **Normal Maps** can be swapped out for **completely different textures**
- You can adjust the **roughness** and **metallic** settings
- You can adjust the size of the texture with the **UV Tiling Old Brick Setting!**

Play around with the UV Tiling settings. Set it to **4.0** and the bricks immediately become **smaller!** Set it to **6.0** and they become **smaller still!**

You now have total control over the size of your textures with easy to use parameters!

Here are some images of different UV settings and texture sizes:

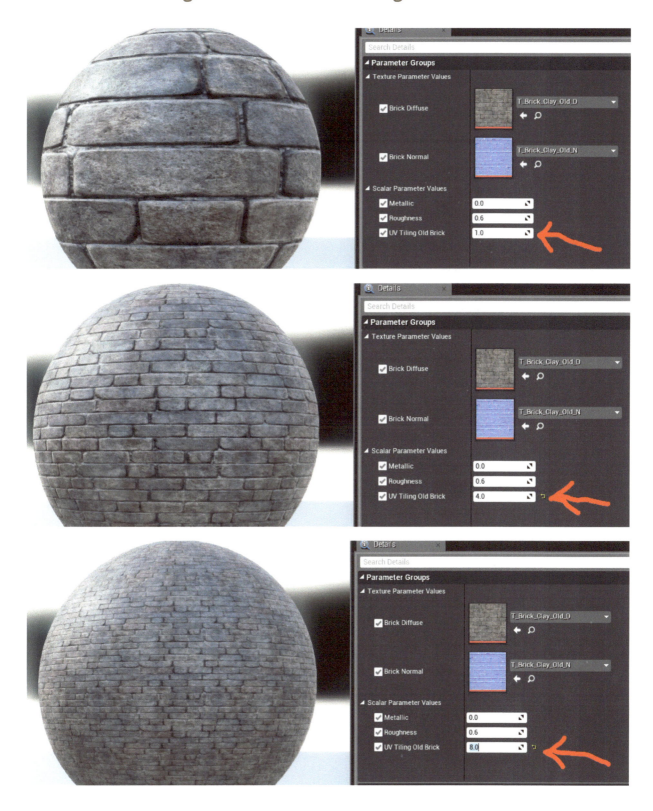

Give yourself a pat on the back - you've just created something that will help you with Materials for a long time to come!

Remember, you can save as many different **Material Instances** as you want, swap out the textures and normal maps and have a collection of different materials in your library.

NOTES:

HOW TO
MAKE A PULSATING, GLOWING MATERIAL
IN UNREAL ENGINE

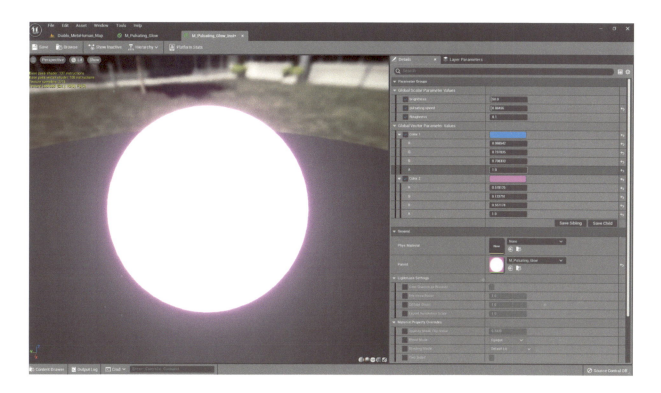

Introduction

Pulsating, glowing materials are one of the most useful things in Unreal Engine! Glowing materials are used in Sci-Fi environments, Fantasy environments, and even for everyday environments such as fluorescent lighting.

In this chapter, we are going to set up a **Master Material** with **Parameters** so that we can easily adjust the **brightness, colors and speed** of the pulsations of the light.

We will then create a **Material Instance** of our Master Material so that the **Parameter Controls** are easily changed, and becomes a drag-and-drop operation.

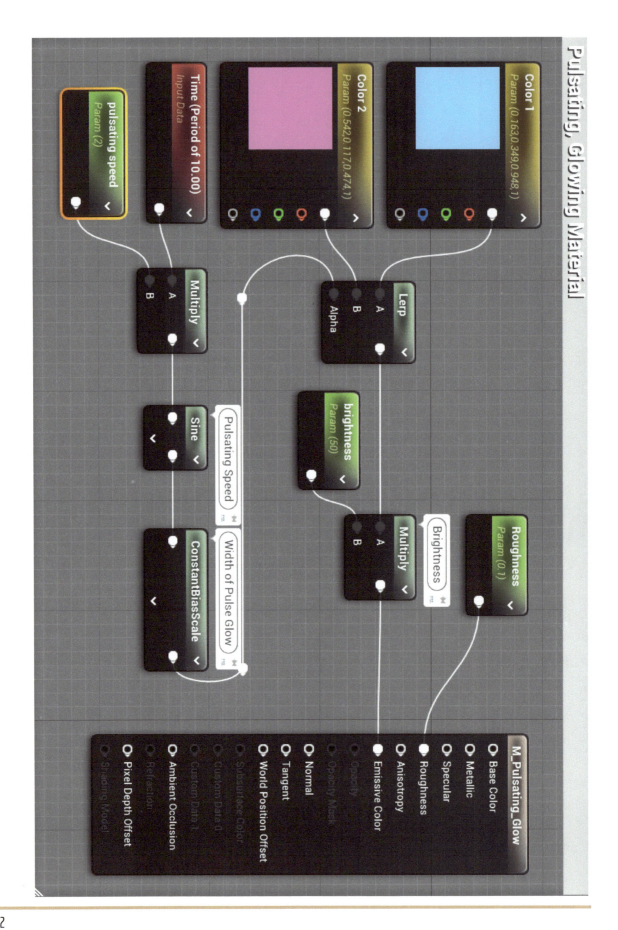

Creating our pulsating, glowing material

First create a new material. You learned how to do this in the prior lesson on texture resizing. Then open up your new material.

We are going to need the following nodes:

- Color nodes (2)
- Multiply nodes (2)
- Sine node (1)
- Time dilation node (1)
- Constant bias scale node (1)
- Roughness node (1)
- Scalar Nodes (2) for brightness and pulsating speed

How To Create Color Nodes

1. In a blank space in your Material editor, **press down the number 3 on your keyboard while clicking your left mouse button.**
2. Name the node **Color 1**
3. Double click in the black square area and change the color from the popup color wheel to a nice **bright blue** (like in the picture)
4. With the node selected, **right click on it and change it into a Parameter** by selecting **'Convert to Parameter'** This will enable us later to have an easy to change control in our Material Instance.
5. Create another color node as you did above, name it **Color 2,** change it to a bright **pink color**, and convert it also to a **Parameter** by right clicking on it and selecting **Convert To Parameter.**
6. Create a **Lerp node** (linear interpolation) by right clicking in the blank area, then in the pop up window start typing **linear**, then scroll down and select **linear interpolation**. This will create the Lerp node. We will hook this up later.
7. Create (2) Multiply nodes by right clicking in the blank area, then in the pop up window start typing **multiply**, then scroll down and select **multiply.**

8. Next create a **time node** by right clicking in the blank area, then in the pop up window start typing **time**, then scroll down and select **time.** Like the image above, go to the **details panel** of the node and **tick the checkbox on** and change the parameter to **10.**

9. Create (3) Scalar Parameters by right clicking in the blank area, then in the pop up window start typing **scalar**, then scroll down and select **scalar parameter.** You can also use the hotkey combination of **typing S** on the keyboard while **clicking your left mouse button.** Name each of these scalar parameters to **pulsating spee**d, **brightness** and **roughness**.

10. Next create a sine node by right clicking in the blank area, then in the pop up window start typing **sine**, then scroll down and select **sine.**

11. Lastly, create a Constant Bias Scale node by right clicking in the blank area, then in the pop up window start typing **constantbiasscale**, then scroll down and select **ConstantBiasScale.**

12. For the next step, select the **pulsating speed node** and make the following changes in the **details tab**:

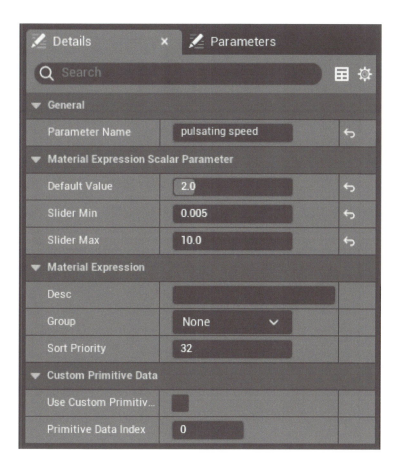

13. Then select the **brightness node** and make the following changes in the **details tab**:

14. Then select the **roughness node** and make the following changes in the **details tab**:

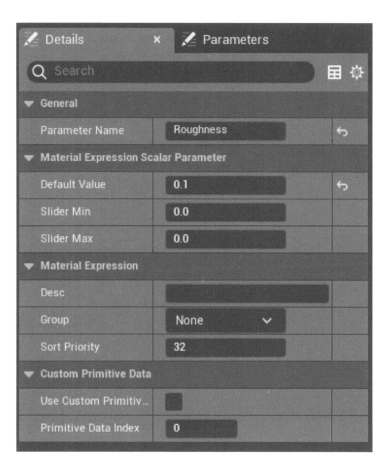

Now let's hook up all the nodes!

Follow the diagram below and hook up all the nodes carefully. Be sure to take your time, because if you get one thing wrong the whole material will not work. You can also use the larger screenshot that is turned sideways a few pages back.

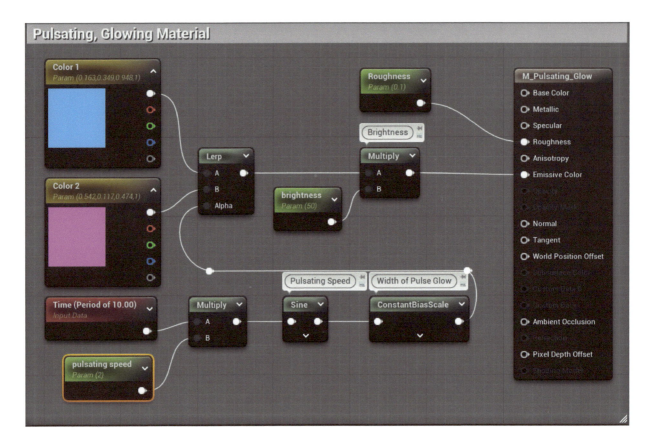

Be sure to save your material!

The final step is to make a **Material Instance** of your Master Material by **selecting** the Master Material, **right clicking** and then selecting **Create Material Instance.** Give it a name that you will remember and that makes sense to you.

I will usually make several Material Instances with different colors and name them accordingly such as **M_Pulsating_Glowing_Green.**

From there it is super easy to just drag-and-drop the Material Instance onto whatever Static Mesh you'd like.

CREATE A DECAL IN UNREAL ENGINE
STEP-BY-STEP INSTRUCTIONS

Introduction

Decals are really handy to break up tileable textures to create a greater sense of realism. With decals, we can add grunge, dirt, discolored paint spots, oil smudges, asphalt road repair, manholes, etc. Here are step-by step instructions to create a simple decal in Unreal Engine 4.

Step One:

Visual Effects > Deferred Decal- Drag Deferred Decal into Scene

Step Two:

Right Click > Create New Material- Name it appropriately and then open it up for editing. I usually create a folder named DECALS and create the material there.

Step Three:

Drag in your textures and maps and connect them like the diagram below: Be sure to use an alpha also, to eliminate the square edged texture and make smooth blended edges in whatever shape you desire. Also be sure to have the correct material settings assigned according to the diagram.

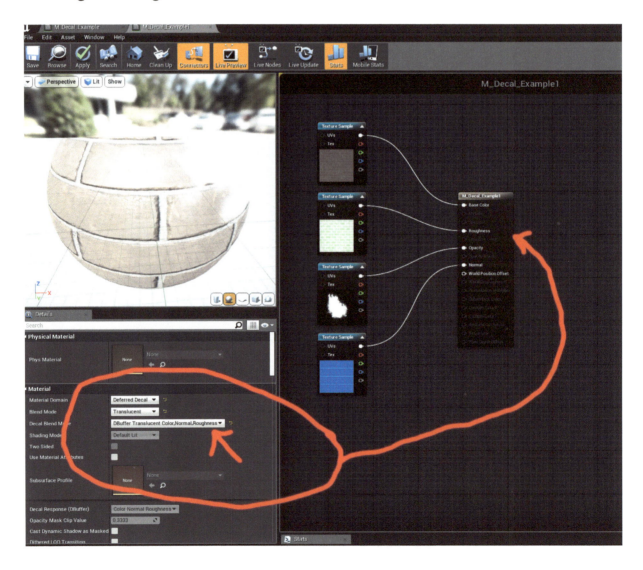

Step Four:

In the World Outliner, click on your Deferred Decal and under the settings drop down Decal Material, and assign the material you just created.

Step Five:

Scale and move your decal- by raising the decal up you can adjust the opacity of the decal so it blends into your scene the way you would like.

This procedure has helped me to break up tileable textures that have a repeating pattern and to achieve more realism. Additional decals can easily be made by duplicating the material and substituting the textures and alphas

CREATE A CAMERA SHAKE
IN UNREAL ENGINE 5

Based on Unreal Engine's Documentation

Camera Shakes

Create camera shake effects in Unreal Engine.

Introduction To Camera Shakes

One of the most effective things you can do in Sequencer to enhance your Cinematics is to create a **CAMERA SHAKE** for your cinematic camera.

You can add a camera shake effect to your cameras using Unreal Engine's Camera Shake Blueprints. This guide provides an overview of how to create a **CameraShakeBase** Blueprint, the type of shakes that are available, and how to play them in Sequencer, Blueprints, and Camera Shake Sources.

Prerequisites

- You have an understanding of **Sequencer** and know how to **Create Camera Animation**.
- You have an understanding of **Blueprint Visual Scripting**.
- If you are using custom sequence-based shakes, then you must have an understanding of **Template Sequences**.

- If you want to test camera shakes in gameplay, you can create a project using the **Third Person Template**.

Camera Shake Creation

To create a shake asset, click **Add/Import** in the **Content Browser** and select **Blueprint Class**. In the next window, locate or search for the **CameraShakeBase** class and click **Select**.

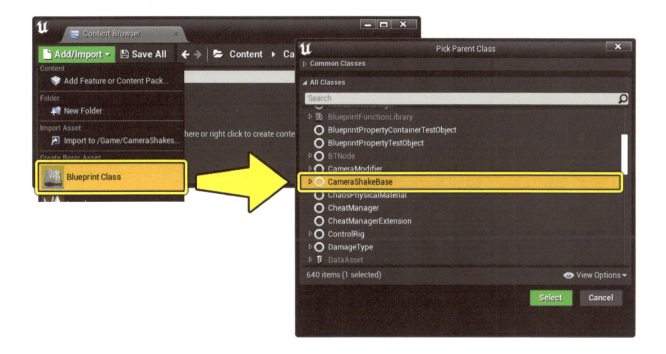

Once the asset is created, name and open it to view the camera shake details.

Details

Camera shake assets have the following base details:

Name	Description
Single Instance	Enabling this will allow only a single instance of this shake to play at a time. Subsequent attempts to play this shake will restart it, instead of layering it additively.

Root Shake Pattern	The **Shake Type** to use.

Root Shake Pattern Types

Shake patterns control the shape and behavior of the camera shake. You are able to select from the following patterns to create a camera shake.

Perlin Noise

Perlin generates noise over time by sampling random points based on a specified amplitude and frequency. These points are blended to by using the **Smootherstep** easing function. Typically, Perlin noise is useful for high-intensity camera shakes such as rumbles or nearby explosions.

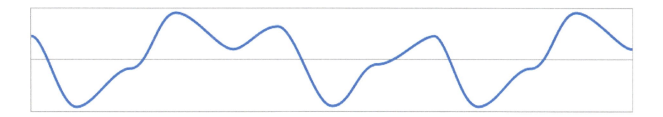

When you select **Perlin Noise Camera Shake Pattern** for your **Root Shake Pattern**, additional details will appear which you can use to control the Perlin noise shake behavior. It is possible to create a shake effect for the location, rotation, and Field of View (FOV) properties of a camera.

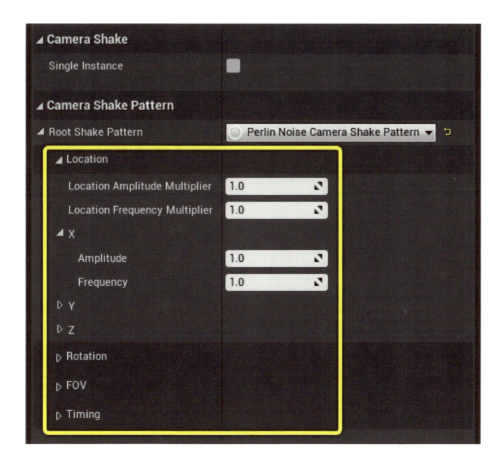

Both **Location** and **Rotation** property categories have their individual axes displayed, and you can expand them to reveal the **Amplitude** and **Frequency** properties.

- **Amplitude** controls the size of the shake pattern. Increasing this will cause the shake on that axis to move a larger distance from the center.
- **Frequency** controls the speed of the shake. Increasing this will cause the shake's movement to appear more rapid.

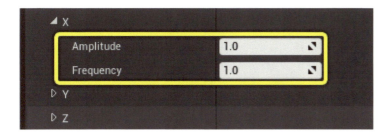

Additionally, you can multiply the combined Amplitude and Frequency results on your Location and Rotation axes by using their **Amplitude** and **Frequency Multiplier**

properties. These properties are useful if you want to make global changes to your shake instead of needing to change each individual axis.

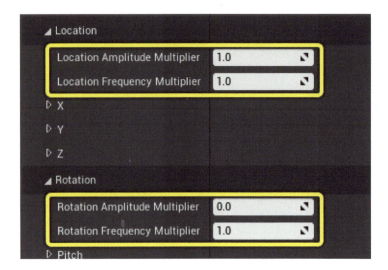

The timing of a shake can be controlled by expanding the **Timing** category.

- **Duration** controls the length of the shake. If it is 0 or less than 0, then the shake will play infinitely.
- **Blend In/Out Time** controls the length of a linear blend at the start and end of the shake. A value of 0 means no blending will occur.

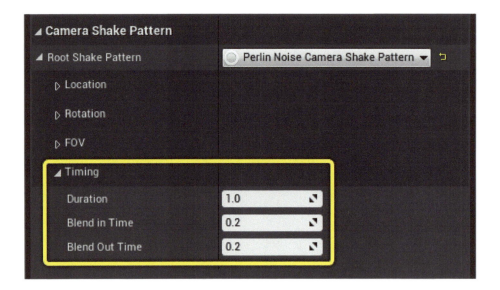

Sinusoidal Wave

Sinusoidal Wave generates noise over time using a continuous wave with smooth periodic oscillation. Typically, wave noise is useful for lower-intensity shakes such as a rocking boat, or a dream-like drifting effect.

When you select **Wave Oscillator Camera Shake Pattern** for your **Root Shake Pattern**, additional details will appear which you can use to control the wave shake behavior. Similar to Perlin noise, it is possible to create a wave shake effect on the location, rotation, and Field of View (FOV) properties of a camera.

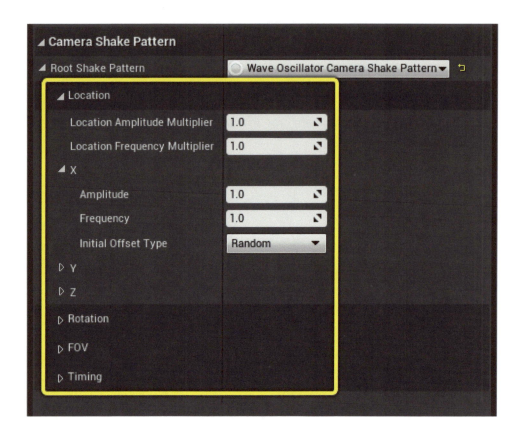

The properties of **Location**, **Rotation**, **FOV**, and **Timing** for Sinusoidal Wave noise are the same as **Perlin Noise**. However, when an axis is expanded, there is an additional property called **Initial Offset Type** from which you can specify if you want your waveform to begin at **Zero** or at a **Random** point along the curve.

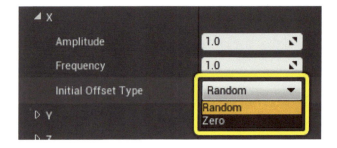

Sequence Shake

Sequence shakes generates shakes using camera animation contained within **Camera Animation Sequences**. Sequence noise is useful in cases where you want full control over the camera's shake style and behavior.

When you select **Sequence Camera Shake Pattern** for your **Root Shake Pattern**, additional details will appear which you can use to select the Camera Animation Sequence asset, and control its behavior. The duration of the shake is based on the length of the camera animation sequence.

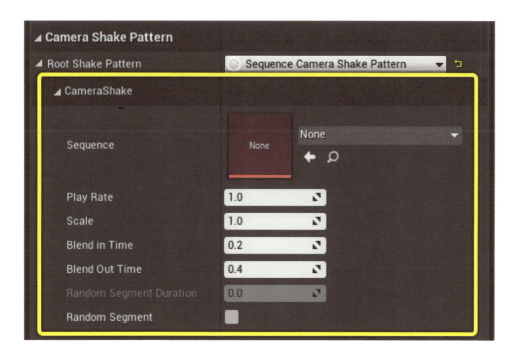

Name	Description
Sequence	Specifies your **Camera Animation Sequence Asset**.
Play Rate	The speed of the shake effect. A value of 1 is normal speed, values less than 1 will play the shake slower, and values higher than 1 will play faster.
Scale	A multiplier applied to the shake intensity. A value of 1 is normal intensity, values less than 1 will be less intense and values higher than 1 will be more intense.
Blend In/Out Time	**Blend In/Out Time** controls the length of a linear blend at the start and end of the shake. A value of 0 means no blending will occur.
Random Segment Duration	The duration of the random segment used if **Random Segment** is enabled.
Random	Enabling this will start playing the shake at a random point in the camera animation sequence. You must also set a value in the

Segme nt	**Random Segment Duration** property to define a new length for the shake. This is useful if you have a very long camera shake animation and want to play random smaller segments from it.

Unlike in typical **Template Sequence** workflows, when creating a Camera Animation Sequence for use as a camera shake pattern, you do not need to set the section to additive.

Composite

Composite shakes enable the combining of **Perlin**, **Wave**, and **Sequence** shakes in a layer system. Using Composite shakes, you can create more varied shakes that include elements from each shake type.

When you select **Composite** Camera Shake Pattern **for your** Root Shake Pattern**, additional details will appear which you can use to add child patterns and layer different shake types together.

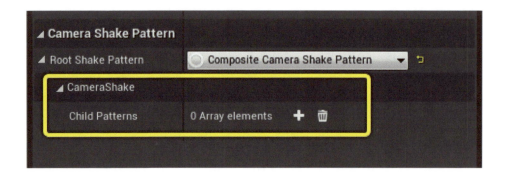

Clicking the **+** button next to **Child Patterns** will add a new shake pattern to the array. You can add as many shake patterns as you want. Each element contains details relevant to that pattern.

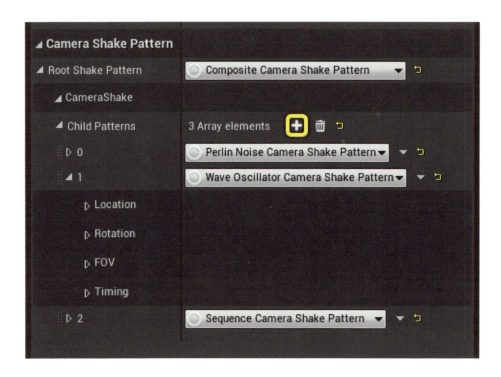

Playing Your Shake

Once you have created your camera shake, there are a couple of ways to play it.

Playing from Sequencer

You can add your shake to a camera in Sequencer by clicking the **+ Track** button on the **Cine Camera Actor** track, and selecting your camera shake asset in the **Camera Shake** menu.

You can also add the shake to the **CameraComponent** track, which produces the same result.

Once added, you can play your sequence to see your shake in action.

The camera shake section contains visualizations for its duration and blend in / out times determined by the Blueprint details. Changing these properties will update the section display.

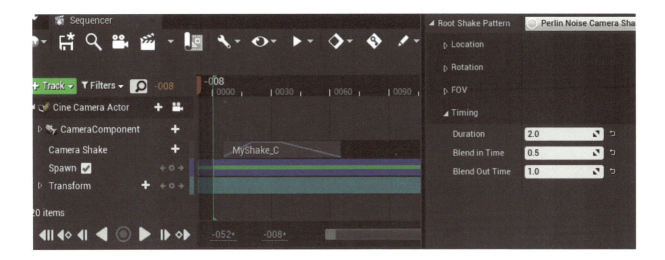

Right-clicking the shake section and navigating to the **Properties** menu will reveal the shake properties in Sequencer.

Name	Description

Shake Class	Specifies the shake Blueprint class to use. You can change this shake to a different asset if another is available.
Play Scale	A global multiplier for the shake intensity. A value of 1 is normal intensity, values less than 1 will be less intense and values higher than 1 will be more intense.
Play Space	Specifies the coordinate space the shake should play in. • **Camera Local** will cause the shake to be relative to the camera's position, making it an additive shake. • **World** will cause the shake coordinates to be relative to the Level's coordinates. • **User Defined** will cause the shake rotational coordinates to be relative to the coordinates specified in **User Defined Play Space**.
User Defined Play Space	When **Play Space** is set to **User Defined**, you can input rotation coordinates here, which are relative to the **World Rotation** coordinates, but with a specified offset.

Playing from Blueprints

You can also play shakes from Blueprints using the **Start Camera Shake** node. The node contains parameters for specifying the **Shake**, **Scale**, and **Play Space**.

The Start Camera Shake function requires a **Player Controller** or a **Camera Shake Source Component** as the target.

Camera Shake Source

The **Camera Shake Source** triggers camera shakes based on the camera's proximity to a location. It also contains controls for the size and radius of the shake influence. You can add it as an **Actor** in your Level, or as a **Component** in Blueprints.

To add a **Camera Shake Source Actor** to your Level, drag it from the **Place Actors** panel into your Level.

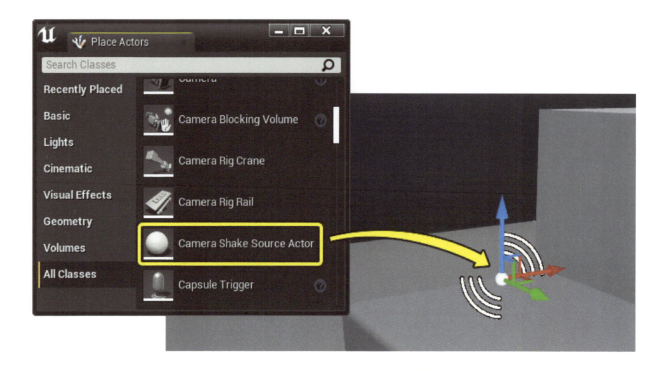

Selecting the Actor or Component will reveal the following details:

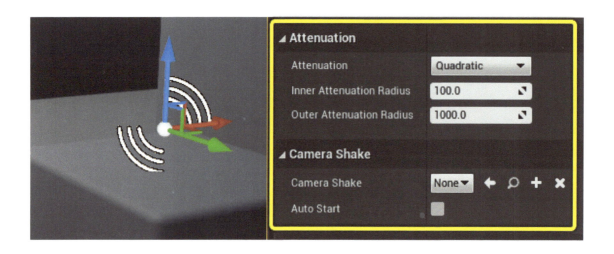

Name	Description
Attenuati on	The falloff curve type as the camera gets closer or further away from the source. This can either be **Quadratic**, which provides

an ease in and out blend, or **Linear**, which provides a linear blend.

Inner Attenuation Radius	The radius from the source in which the shake will play at its full intensity.
Outer Attenuation Radius	The radius from the source in which the shake will no longer be visible. The shake will blend its intensity between the outer and inner radius as the camera moves between them.
Camera Shake	The shake Blueprint class to use.
Auto Start	Enabling this will cause the shake to automatically start when playing the game.

Looping Shake Example

You can quickly create a source shake effect by doing the following:

1. In the **Camera Shake Blueprint**, set all **Timing** properties to 0. This will make the shake loop indefinitely with no blending. Also ensure you have set an appropriate amplitude and frequency on your axes so that the shake is visible.

2. Assign the Blueprint to the camera shake source **Camera Shake** property, and enable **Auto Start**.

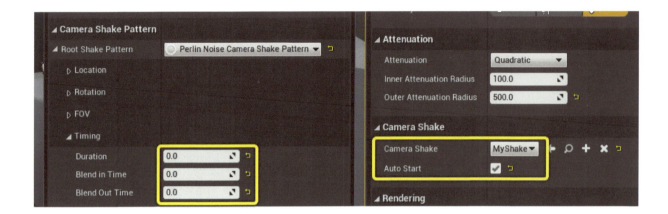

Now when you play the game and approach the source point, you should see the shake blend on and off as the camera enters the influence of the camera shake source.

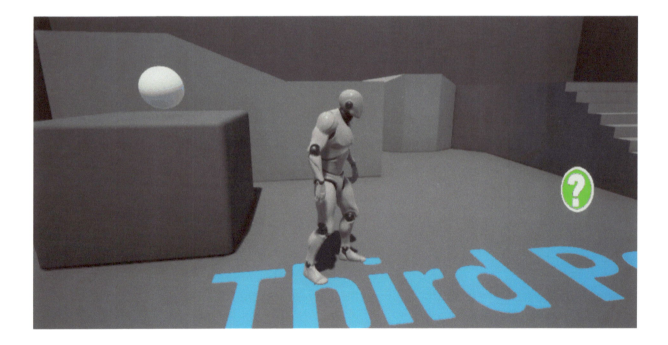

Camera Shake Previewer

The Camera Shake Previewer can be used to preview **Camera Shake Sources** in the editor without needing to start the game or simulation.

To open the previewer, navigate to Unreal Editor's main menu and select **Window > Camera Shake Previewer**.

In order for camera shakes to play in the editor, you will need to enable **Allow Camera Shakes** in the viewport options menu.

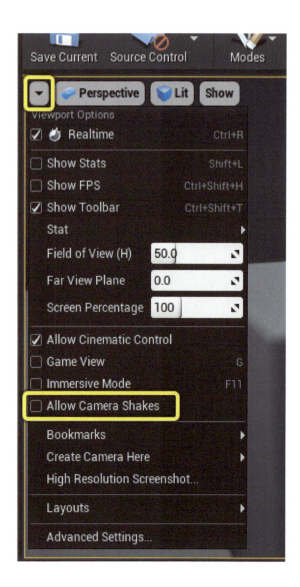

Next, select the shake source entry you want to preview and click **Play/Stop Selected** to enable the shake preview. You can also click **Play/Stop All** if you want to preview multiple sources at once. Once it is playing, you can move the editor's camera towards the source and see the shake effect.

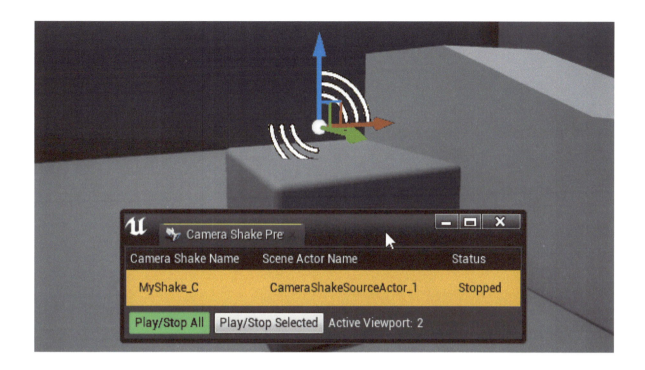

Camera Shake Pre

Camera Shake Name	Scene Actor Name	Status
MyShake_C	CameraShakeSourceActor_1	Stopped

Play/Stop All Play/Stop Selected Active Viewport: 2

Congratulations, you did it! Give yourself a pat on the back because this is something that will enhance your cinematics and animations in a big way.

HOW TO

ANIMATE THE VIGILANTE
HELICOPTER
IN UNREAL ENGINE

Introduction To Animating The Vigilante Helicopter

Important: These military assets will only work in Unreal Engine Version 4.27 - However, you can migrate them over into Unreal Engine 5

Link for Helicopter Asset:

https://www.unrealengine.com/marketplace/en-US/product/heli-uh60a-west

(these are FREE assets provided by Vigilante)

In this tutorial we are going to learn how to get your **Vigilante Helicopter** to animate and fly in **Sequencer.**

We will animate our **Vigilante Helicopter's** main rotor blade, rear rotor blade, door, ground dust, and exhaust flumes. We will animate the helicopter so it takes off from the ground and then returns to the ground in a loop.

We will then create a cinematic camera, add it to Sequencer, create some nice looking depth of field and then "real-time" render the video out of Unreal Engine. The steps to achieve this are pretty straightforward but are not covered in the documentation at all. I had to search far and wide to put the pieces together, along with a lot of trial and error.

Soon you will have your **Vigilante Helicopter** flying however you wish!

Keep in mind the steps for all the other military vehicles are the same. We are starting with the Helicopter because it is one of the most difficult.

Ready to get started? Let's begin!

These are the first steps:

- Create a new **4.27 Unreal Project** and name it as you wish.
- Add the **Heli UH60A** asset from the Unreal Marketplace to your project
- Add the **Control Rig Plugin** (and restart Unreal Engine)

  (The Control Rig plugin is necessary in order to animate the helicopter's individual parts, as you will soon see)

Step 1: Create A New Level

Name this Level whatever you choose. I usually will create a new folder in the **Content Browser** with sub-folders - Levels, Meshes, Blueprints, Cinematics/Sequencer, Audio, etc.

Step 2: Add the BP_Heli UH60A Blueprint Asset To Your Level

This can be found under **VigilanteContent > Vehicles > West_Heli_UH60A.** Click and drag the asset into your Scene/Level. Be sure that it is the BP version (Blueprint version) because that's the one that has the dust and exhaust particles we will need later.

SIDE NOTE: I will usually scale the floor to a larger size such as **10**. I also usually select the main **Light Source**, make it **'moveable'** and increase the amount to **10** in the details panel so it is easier to set up the scene.

Step 3: Create A New Sequence (Level Sequence)

Name this Sequence anything you'd like.

Step 4: Add the Helicopter To Sequencer

With your Helicopter asset selected, either drag it into the Sequencer window or use the **GREEN +Track button** to find the Helicopter and add it to the Sequencer.

Step 5: Add the Control Rig FK Editing Controls To The Helicopter

This is where the magic begins and will give you the ability to animate every moving part on this cool Helicopter asset!

- Select the BP
- Right click and a menu will popup
- Go to **Control Rig > Edit With FK Control Rig** and select it. This will convert to FK Control Rig and Add a track for it
- Another menu will popup **(Options for baking).** Leave settings at the default and click **CREATE**

Now you will have a new track under **BP_West_Heli_UH60A.** Click on the **little arrow** to the left of the track and it will expand into numerous sub tracks containing all the parts that can be animated. For this tutorial we will be interested in two objects: the **main rotor** and the **rear rotor**.

Step 6: Create Keyframes for Main Rotor & Rear Rotor

Be sure you have the **FKControlRig** selected in your Sequencer and then in the search bar at the top of the Sequencer, type in **rotor_jnt.** This will bring up only the two controls we want to animate, **rotor_jnt** and **rearRotor_joint**.

- Select the **rotor_jnt**
- Expand the rotor_jnt, then drag select all the keyframes in the **Sequencer** and **delete them**
- Select the **Rotation: Yaw** and make sure the setting is at **0**, then **create a keyframe at the beginning of the animation** (tiny + sign on same track of Rotation: Yaw)
- **Bottom right of Sequencer**, change the length of the animation to 500 frames and then drag the red end line to match 500 frames
- **Move the playhead forward 10 frames**, change the setting of the **Rotation: Yaw** to **360**, and **create a keyframe**
- Select the **first keyframe** by clicking on it, and then **RIGHT-CLICK** to bring up the menu. Under **KEY INTERPOLATION**, select **LINEAR (the triangle icon)**. Do the same with the other keyframe
- Next, **RIGHT CLICK on an empty part in the same track and a menu will come up**. Select **Post-Infinity >Cycle**. What this will do is repeat the animation throughout the entire animation without having to manually create them. **AWESOME, right?**
- **Now do the same steps for the rearRotor_jnt, but use the Rotation: Roll setting**

Step 7: Animate The Side Door Opening & Closing

- Search in the Sequencer search bar for **rt_rear_door_jnt**
- Click on the **little arrow** to expand the settings
- Select **Location.X**
- **Delete** existing keyframes

- Set keyframe at **-7 at beginning of animation**
- Set keyframe at **-7 at end of animation** (so it will loop seamlessly)
- Set keyframe at around **-140 in the middle of the animation**

Step 8: Animate The Helicopter Taking Off and Landing

- Search for **root_jnt** in the Sequencer search bar
- Expand the little arrow to expose the settings
- Select **Location.Z** and create a keyframe of **0 at the beginning of the animation**
- Select **Location.Z** and create a keyframe of **0 at the end of the animation**
- Select **Location.Z** and create a keyframe of **600 at frame 250 of the animation**

  (Use your own settings according to your needs)

Step 9: Animate Slight Rotations In Helicopter Flight

- Search for the **root_jnt** in the Sequencer search bar
- Using the above methods, set keyframes for **Rotation.Roll, Rotation.Pitch** during the animation. **Remember to set the beginning keyframe and end keyframe at 0** so it will loop nicely without a glitch

Step 10: Animate Ground Dust From Rotors

Step 11: Animate Exhaust Heat Waves From Engines

Step 12: Add A Cinematic Camera To The Sequencer

Step 13: Render Out Your Video

Give yourself a big pat on the back! You've learned something that can help you in future animations with all kinds of different assets!

And remember - most importantly, HAVE FUN!

If you've enjoyed this tutorial and would like to learn more, check out my Unreal Engine Courses:

https://michael-ricks.com/

HOW TO

ANIMATE DAZ GENESIS 3 CHARACTERS
IN Mixamo &
UNREAL ENGINE

Introduction

Unlike the Genesis 2 Characters that can be exported as an FBX file with no revisions, the Genesis 3 Characters have had their rigging changed to where the Mixamo program will not recognize the skeletal structure and rejects it.

The following tutorial will show a way around this, so that you can use the Genesis 3 characters in Mixamo and Unreal Engine 4 - it just requires a different workflow.

Open up a scene with your DAZ Genesis 3 Character

Once you have your scene open, select your character in the scene panel and lower the resolution from HIGH RESOLUTION MESH to BASE RESOLUTION. This is very important, so be sure not to omit this step or your character will not load into Mixamo. It will only accept the base resolution mesh at this time. You will not lose your details, as they will come across in the normal map when you set up the materials in Unreal Engine 4.

Export your character in Wavefront OBJ format

Go to File > Export and when the dialogue window opens select Wavefront OBJ from the options in the drop down menu. Name your character and select "Save." Another dialogue window will open. Use the following settings:

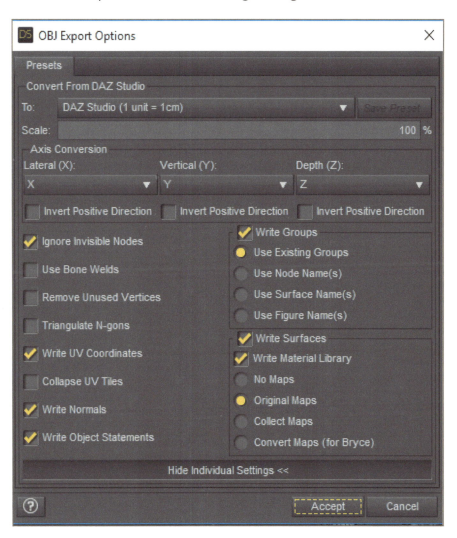

Delete your Genesis 3 original character from the scene

Now Go to **File > Import** and bring in your Wavefront OBJ character that you *just saved.* What we have done is eliminate all the bones and rigging in the character so that there will be no problems when we go to import it into Mixamo.

Export your Genesis 3 Wavefront OBJ character as an FBX file

Go to **File > Export** and select **FBX** from the drop down choices. As you did before, choose a name for your file/character and select "Save." A dialogue window will open - use the following settings:

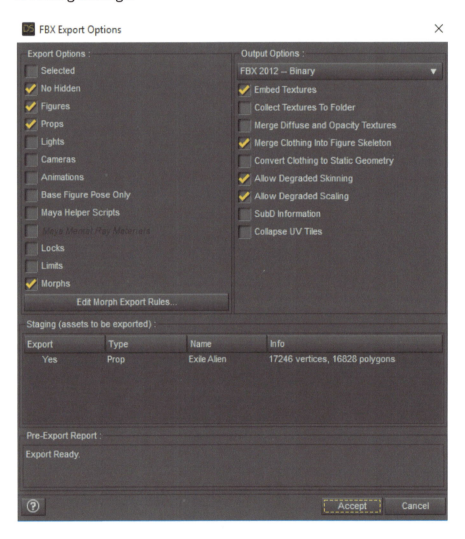

Go to www.mixamo.com - you will need to register for an Adobe account if you don't already have one in order to use Mixamo.

Log into your account and you will be brought to this page:

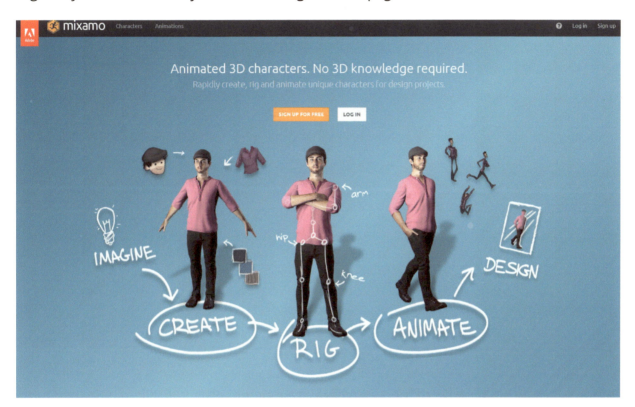

Thousands of motion-capture animations

At this time the Adobe Mixamo service along with all of it's animations are available free of charge making this an unbelievable goldmine for artists, game designers and animators! In addition to using your own characters, there are over 70 characters on the website that are available for your use.

The following steps will cover how to upload your Genesis 3 character to Mixamo, how to demo and add animations, and how to export these animations embedded into your character ready for use in Unreal Engine 4.

Upload your character to Mixamo

Mixamo has a drag and drop feature - simply drag your FBX file into the dotted window as shown in the screenshot below. Or you can browse for your file in the normal manner. As your file is being uploaded you will see a green status bar as it progresses.

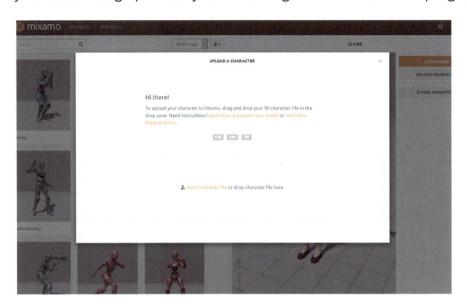

Process your character

Mixamo has an amazing set of tools.   It will take a moment after your file is uploaded to process your character. You will see this screen after processing. Click "Next."

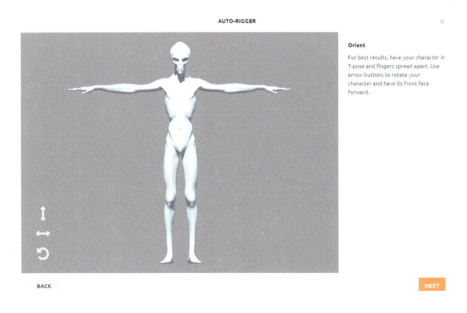

Prepare your character for the Mixamo auto-rig tool

You will then see your character in a T-Pose ready to position markers on the mesh.

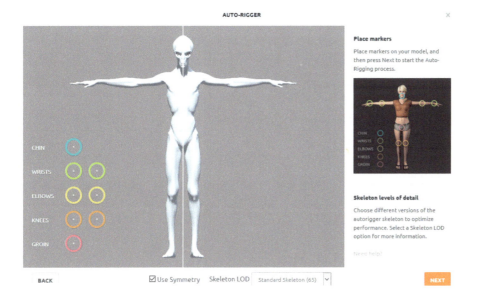

Position the colored markers

Drag and drop the colored circles to the appropriate areas. The chin, the wrists, the elbows, the knees and the groin. A small, zoomed in window will assist you with the placement. When you are finished, press the "Next" button.

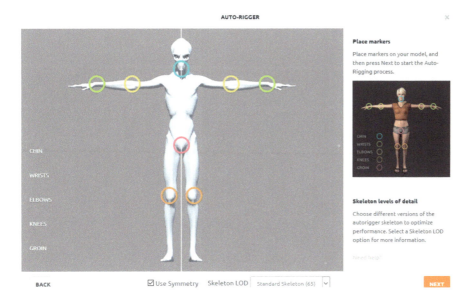

Mixamo will now automatically create a skeleton & rig for your character

This process usually takes less than 2 minutes - your character will be slowly spinning during this process. It's really an amazing thing to watch.

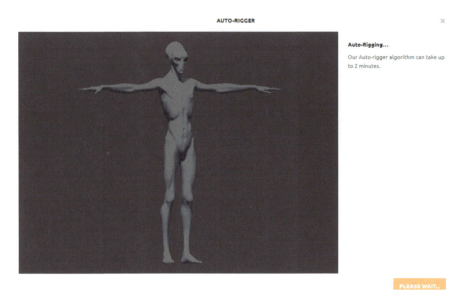

Your character is rigged and moving!

Your Genesis 3 character will be rigged and moving around with a default animation applied to it.

How To Get DAZ Studio

Genesis 8 Characters
To Mixamo, Then To
Unreal Engine

Step 1: Import your DAZ Genesis 8 Character Into DAZ Studio

> ***VERY IMPORTANT STEP:*** *Click on your character in the scene panel and lower the resolution from HIGH RESOLUTION to BASE RESOLUTION by clicking on the Parameters tab and then mesh resolution. At this time, Mixamo will not accept the high resolution mesh, only the base mesh. You will not lose your details as they will come across in the normal map when we set up the materials in Unreal Engine 4.*

Step 2: Export your character in Wavefront OBJ format:
File > Export. Dialog window will open - select from the drop down menu. Name your character and then select "Save."
A Dialog Window will open.Use the following settings:

Step 3: Delete your DAZ Genesis 8 character from the scene.

Step 4:   Import your exported OBJ Genesis 8 character.

Step 4A: Add only the **diffuse materials** to your character. Important: If you add any other textures such as normal, roughness, etc - **Mixamo will reject your character import.**

Step 4B: Export your Genesis 8 character as an Autodesk FBX file:

(File > Export: Select FBX from the drop down choices).

As before, choose a name, and select "Save."
        A Dialog Window will open.Use the following settings:

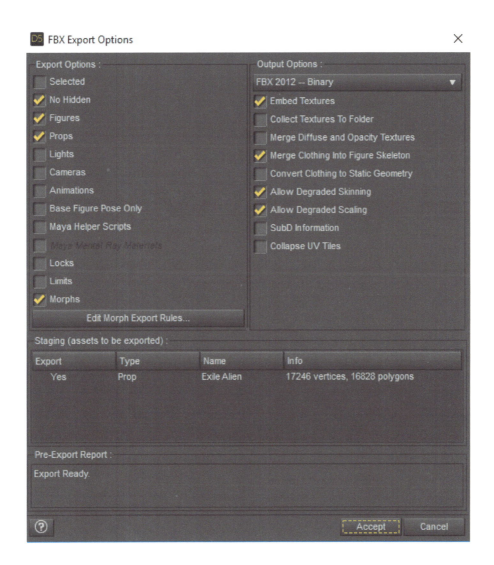

Step 5:   Go to www.mixamo.com - you will need an Adobe account if you don't already have one in order to use Mixamo. Log in to your account.

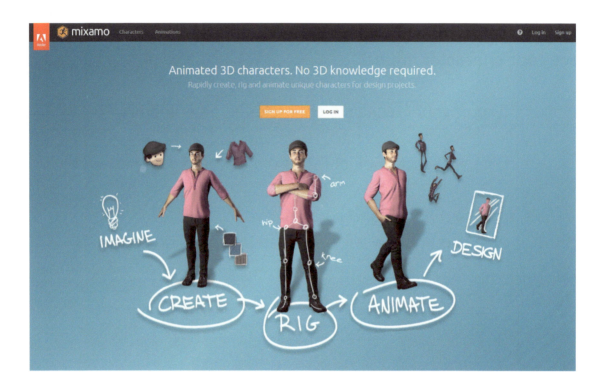

Step 6:   Upload your character *(you can drag your file to the dotted line area if you wish)*

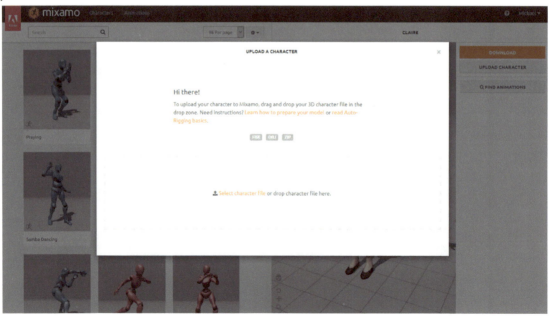

Step 7: Prepare your character for Auto-Rig. You will see your character imported. Click the "Next" button.

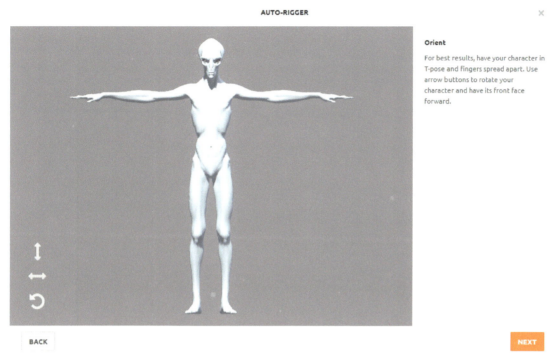

Step 8: This screen is where you will prepare your character for Mixamo's Auto-Rig Tool.

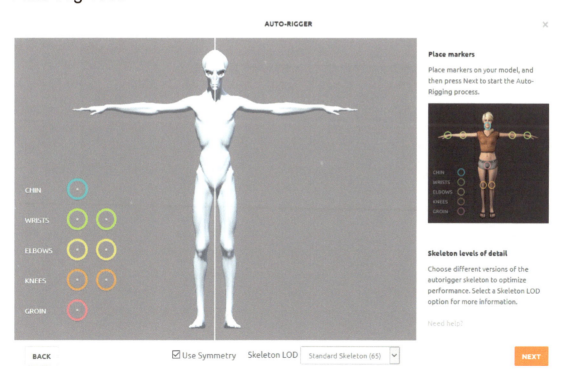

Step 9: Position the colored circles by dragging them to the chin, wrists, Elbows, knees and groin. Then press the "Next" button.

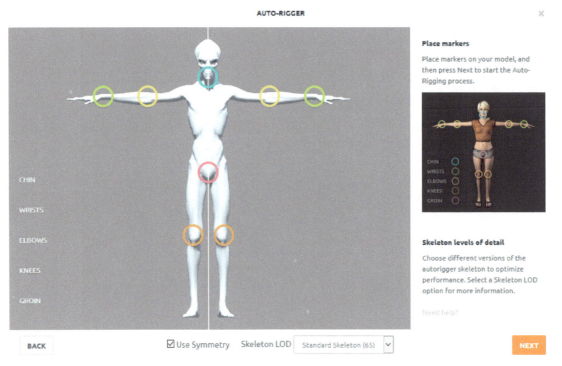

Step 10: Mixamo will automatically create a skeletal rig for your character while you watch. It usually takes less than 2 minutes. (Your character will be rotating during this process)

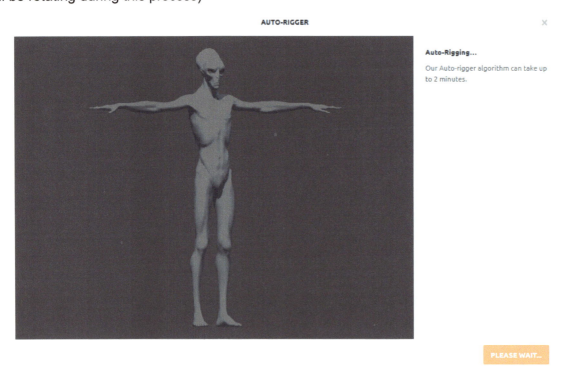

Step 11: When Mixamo completes creating your rig you will see the next screen, with a default animation applied. Your character will be looking around.

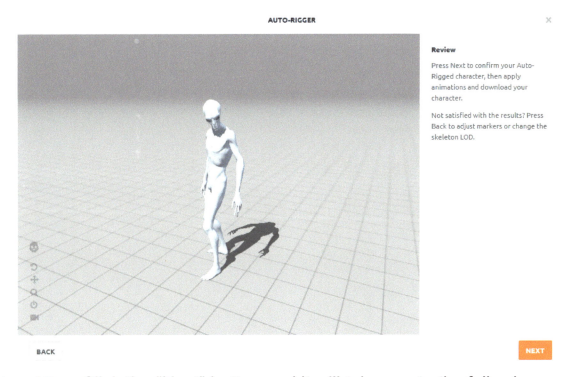

Step 12: Click the "Next" button and it will take you to the following screen:

CHANGE CHARACTER   ✕

Your 3D character has been uploaded.

Proceed with this new character?

Your previous character will not be saved.

☐ Do not show this warning next time   NEXT

Step 13:   Click "Next" and it will take you to the following screen:

(Your character will be in a T-Pose, ready to have an animation applied)

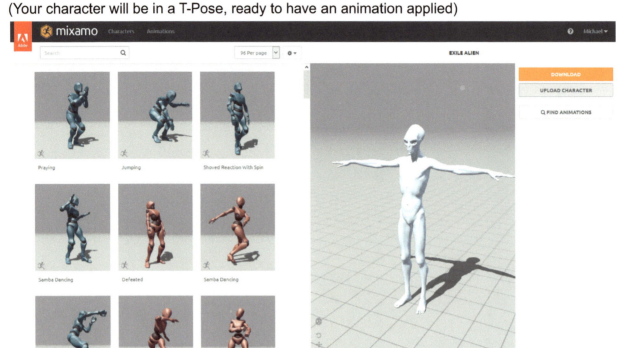

Step 14:   Apply an animation to your character by clicking on one of the animated previews to the left of your character. There are thousands of professionally created motion-capture animations for you to use. At this time, Mixamo is free to use and download all the animations you would like. You can also search for specific animations like "dance," "fight," "lying down," etc. It's a blast to apply different animations to your character!

You can click in the larger animation window where your character is and rotate the view in real time during the animation. When you find an animation you like, select the orange DOWNLOAD button.

IMPORTANT: *It is necessary for you to download your first animation **WITH SKIN**, so you have the mesh attached to the rig/skeleton Mixamo created for you. After that you can download subsequent animations without skin and apply the animations to your skeleton in Unreal Engine 4. This saves a lot of time during the importing process later in Unreal Engine 4.*

Step 15: Download your character with animation. Select the download button and choose with skin as mentioned above. Export as FBX. The screen will look like this:

DOWNLOAD SETTINGS

Format

| FBX(.fbx) | ⌄ |

Skin

| With Skin | ⌄ |

Frames per Second

| 30 | ⌄ |

Keyframe Reduction

| none | ⌄ |

CANCEL   DOWNLOAD

Now you're ready to import your character along with the Mixamo animations attached into Unreal Engine 4. Let the fun begin!

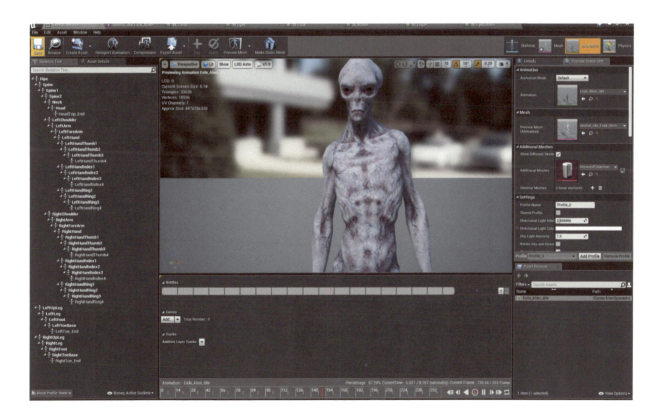

Step 16: Import your file into Unreal Engine 4. Use the following settings:

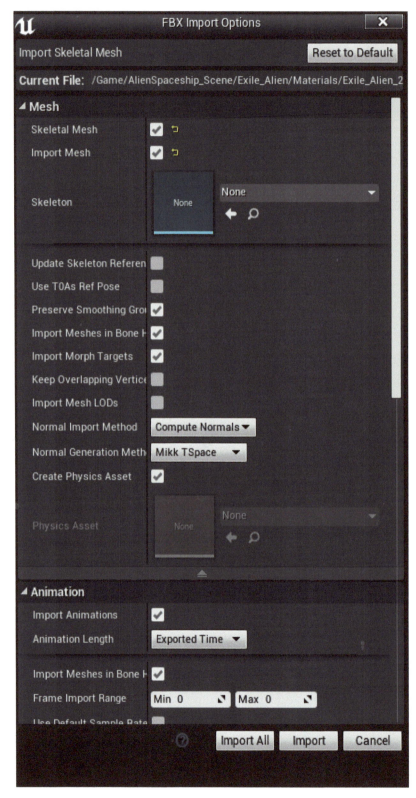

Note: In many cases you may need to import your character at 0.01 scale or it will be gigantic!

Step 17:   Now that your character is imported into Unreal Engine 4, all you need to do is drag the animation thumbnail into your scene and hit "Play." Your character will come to life with the animation you got from Mixamo!

SUMMARY:

The next step will be to import your texture maps, normal maps, roughness, metallic, etc - then create and assign the materials to your character.

APPLY ROOT ANIMATION TO YOUR CHARACTERS
IN UNREAL ENGINE

Introduction

You know the situation - you import your character with motion-capture, he takes two steps and then the animation snaps back to frame 1.   We're going to cover step-by-step **how to extend the animation** and get your character walking or running for as long as you like and covering ground in the process, not just running in place.

We're going to use the included **Mannequin Robot Character** that UE4 provides. Here we go!

Import Starter Animation Pack from the Unreal Marketplace

From the Epic Launcher, go to the Marketplace and search for the **Animation Starter Pack**. It's free and contains a ton of free animations along with the UE4 Robot Mannequin.

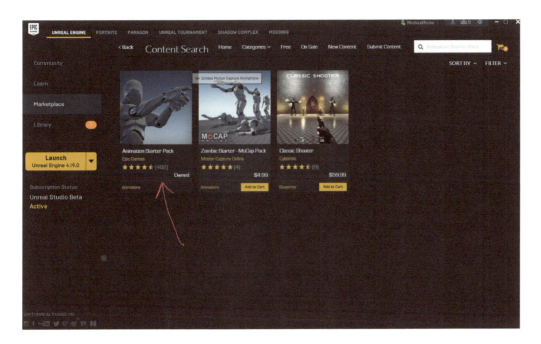

Add the Animation Starter Pack to your scene:

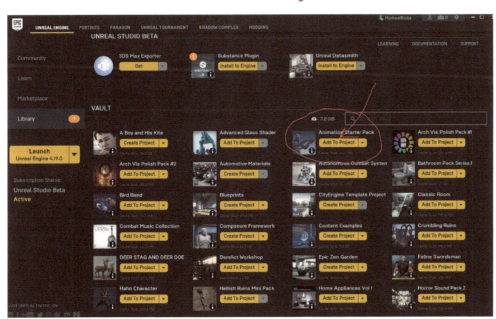

Let's pick out our animation

Click on the **AnimStarterPack** folder, and type 'jog' into the search field. It will narrow down your search to make it easier to find the animation. Click on the **Jog_Fwd_Rifle** animation and select duplicate from the popup menu to make a copy of the animation. Rename it **Jog_Fwd_Rifle_Rootmotion.**

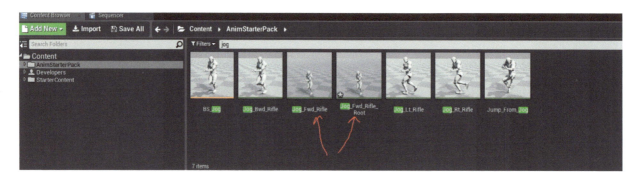

Now we're going to revise the animation

Double click on your new **Jog_Fwd_Rifle_Root** animation. Notice that the animation has **44 frames** and is a smooth looping animation with the character running in place. This works great for game characters, but for cinematics what if we want the character to move and cover actual ground? And without slipping and sliding feet! Fortunately Unreal Engine 4 has a solution buried within its powerful toolset.

Let's add some root motion to the animation

In the skeleton tree menu to the far left, click on the **root bone** to select it. Be sure your scrubber is on frame 0 in the timeline. Up in the top menu, click on the Key button to create a keyframe at that position.

Next, move your scrubber to the end of the timeline (frame 44) and then move your character forward (be sure the tool is in translate mode, not rotate or scale) to the far left of the viewport window. You will see a line indicating the motion. Click the key button to create a keyframe.   It should look something like this:

Let's play the animation

Very cool! Our character jogs forward about 4 steps and then returns to the starting point to begin again. But what if we want our character to go a longer distance? What if we want him to run across the entire surface? Can we just add frames to the end of the animation and drag the root bone out? Unfortunately not, the cycle of jogging will end after frame 44. We need to find a way to loop or extend the jogging animation. We will do that by creating an **Animation Composite**, which will allow us to blend multiple animations together.

How to create an Animation Composite

Go back to the **Content Browser** and in the animation folder we are going to create an **Animation Composite** by **right clicking on an empty space,** go up to **Animation**, then when the menu expands select **Animation Composite.** Another window will open up and ask you to pick a skeleton. Pick the **UE4_Mannequin_Skeleton.** The window will close and you will see your new Animation JogComposite highlighted, ready for you to rename. Let's rename it **Jog_Root_Motion. Double click on this.** A new window will open up for you to create your Animation Composite - it will look like this:

Compositing the animation & extending the jog cycle

Next go to the Asset Browser to the right of the screen, click and drag the Jog_Fwd_Rifle animation to the composite layer (the top layer) and release. It will turn green. Do this again, but drop it onto the second track below the first one. Do this one more time on the top track again. As you can see, each time we do this the animation is extended longer. Press play and you will see that the character is now jogging in place for 128 frames. But there is no forward movement and we cannot do that here. First we must record this animation as a new one.

Recording the animation to prepare for root motion

This part is a bit tricky, but after you do it a few times its a breeze. Press play to start the animation (so the character is jogging in place). Next, press the red record button down in the far right corner of the timeline. A menu will open up asking you to save the animation and give it a name. Let's call it **JogLongDistance**. Now, when you hit OK, the menu will close and the animation will be recording in real time. Go ahead and let it record for about 10 seconds or so (there is a timer in the viewport showing you the recording process). Then press the red record key again to stop the recording.

Adding the forward motion to your character

Find your **JogLongDistance** animation in the content browser and **double click** on it to open it. You will see that your character is running in place. Press the **pause button** to stop the animation. Make sure you are on **frame 0** of the animation in the timeline and then select the **root bone** in the **skeleton tree**. With the translate tool, move your character back all the way to the end of the surface to the left of the viewport. We want him to have lots of space to run. Press the **Key button** in the top menu to create a keyframe.

Next, move your slider in the timeline to the **end of the animation**. Move your character forward, all the way to the other end of the surface to the left of the viewport. Click on the **Key button** again to create a keyframe there.

Now put your slider at **frame 0** in the timeline and press the play button. Your character is now jogging from one end of the surface to the other! Be sure to save your animation by pressing the save button in the top left corner.

Congratulations, you did it! Give yourself a pat on the back because this is something that has frustrated animators for quite some time.

The **Animation Composite** feature in UE4 is very powerful. Keep in mind you can put different animations in there such as a jump, turn, roll or whatever by using this same procedure.

I hope you've enjoyed this book and that it helped out a bit. Have fun animating and contact me if you have any questions!

Don't forget to join the Facebook Group I created just for you at: https://www.facebook.com/groups/UnrealEngineTraining/

Warm regards,

Michael Ricks
Unreal Engine Courses: https://michael-ricks.com
Facebook: https://www.facebook.com/ricks.michael
Facebook Group: Mike's Unreal Engine Training Group:
https://www.facebook.com/groups/UnrealEngineTraining/
Email: mikericks@yahoo.com

www.ingramcontent.com/pod-product-compliance
Lightning Source LLC
LaVergne TN
LVHW060201050326
832903LV00016B/335